To Annie, Sophie,
Ralph, and Nellie, my
runway-perfect dog
—DB

To Irene & Galina,
who taught me to play
dress-up for life
—MD

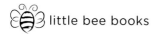 little bee books

An imprint of Bonnier Publishing USA
251 Park Avenue South, New York, NY 10010
Text copyright © 2018 by Deborah Blumenthal
Illustrations copyright © 2018 by Masha D'yans
All rights reserved, including the right of reproduction
in whole or in part in any form. Little Bee Books is a
trademark of Bonnier Publishing USA, and associated colophon is
a trademark of Bonnier Publishing USA.
Manufactured in China   HUH 0618
First Edition   10 9 8 7 6 5 4 3 2 1
Library of Congress Cataloging-in-Publication Data
Names: Blumenthal, Deborah, author. | D'yans, Masha, illustrator.
Title: Polka dot parade / by Deborah Blumenthal; illustrated by Masha D'yans.
Description: First edition. | New York, NY: Little Bee Books, [2018]
Includes bibliographical references. | Identifiers: LCCN 2017023554
Subjects: LCSH: Cunningham, William J. | Photographers—United States—Biography—Juvenile literature. |
Fashion photography—Juvenile literature. | Fashion—New York (State)—New York—Juvenile literature.
Classification: LCC TR140.C778 B58 2018 | DDC 770.92—dc23
LC record available at https://lccn.loc.gov/2017023554

ISBN 978-1-4998-0664-9

littlebeebooks.com
bonnierpublishingusa.com

POLKA DOT PARADE

A BOOK ABOUT BILL CUNNINGHAM

WORDS:
DEBORAH BLUMENTHAL

PICTURES:
MASHA D'YANS

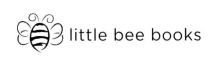

little bee books

Bill Cunningham cycled
through New York City,
dawn to dark.

He wore a blue French
worker's jacket,
tan pants, and
black sneakers.

A camera was slung
around his neck,
and his twinkling eyes
were forever searching.

"He who seeks beauty
will find it," Bill said.

And he did.

He found it in
first-nighter galas and
life on the streets.

He found "sheer poetry"
in the drape of
an evening dress,

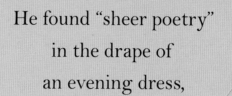

delight
in the swoosh of a
knife-pleated skirt,
and sartorial splendor
in Jazz Age garb.

He found it in lush Hermès bags,
fanny packs, ginghams, plaids,
and grays "with a dash
of sapphire or violet."

He even marveled at
fancy-pants dog clothes: coats,
sweaters, and jeweled leashes.

"I don't really
see people,
I see clothes,"
Bill said.

He snapped picture after picture,
then placed them together
on *New York Times* pages,
like squares on a story quilt.

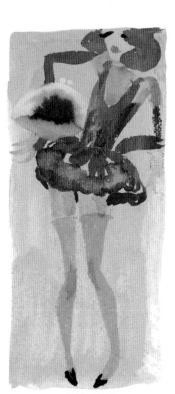

Pictures were his words,
fashion his language.

"Fashion is the armor
to survive the reality
of everyday life," Bill said.

It wasn't about being rich or poor. It was about STYLE.

"A lot of people have taste," Bill said,
"but they don't have the daring to be creative."

For Bill, clothes told stories
not only about the people who wore them,
but also about the times they lived in.

Because like tattletales,
clothes tell secrets.

After working as a hatmaker, Bill turned to writing about fashion.

Then he taught himself to take pictures.

Pictures of those who *made* fashion, not followed it.

Those who weren't afraid to look silly.

People who looked like leopards in their leopard prints, cool cats in their hats, dudes in dots and spots.

Those who didn't give a hoot if others stared or laughed.

Fashion, after all, is about being true
to yourself, whoever you are.

It's about freedom.

Seeking beauty, Bill
went to posh parties and
to Fashion Week in Paris.

But sometimes he just stood
outside in New York, waiting
for beauty to pass him by.

Bill had a favorite Manhattan street corner:
Fifth Avenue and Fifty-Seventh Street.

"My whole thing is to be invisible," he said.
"You get more natural pictures that way too."

He'd snap yellow handbags
in the autumn gold of
ginkgo trees in Central Park.

He'd shoot geometric patterns and
stripes in stark black and white—
"an unbeatable combination."

He'd photograph New Yorkers in the rain
doing puddle-jumping dances in
their thousand-dollar shoes.

Bill would develop his film at a one-hour photo center and then go to the office
to pore over his work like a jeweler examining Colombian emeralds.

"I don't work,"
Bill said.

"I only know
how to have
fun every day."

Bill rode around New York City on his bicycle,
braving snow, wind, and ice.

Many times, his bicycle got stolen or dented by cars.
So he bought another. And another. Thirty in all.

Bill's private life was sparse.

A small apartment.

No kitchen
because he didn't cook.

No television
because he didn't watch.

Not even a private bath.

He slept on a narrow bed.

All around him,
dozens of cabinets
held thousands and thousands
of his photographs.

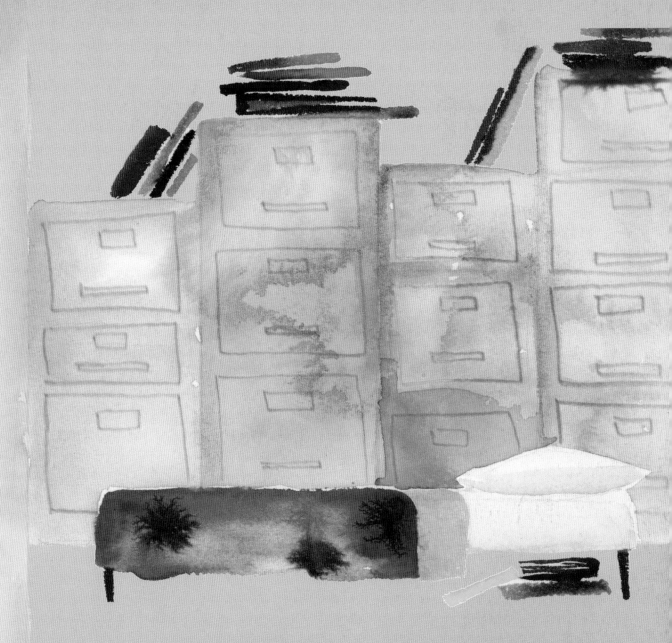

Everyone Bill met wanted
him to take a picture of them.

But he wouldn't.

He'd smile and move on,
fixing his lens on people
who looked special to him
in a way only he understood.

Everyone loved Bill
because he loved life
and all the fantastical
paths it took people down.

In 2008, the French government gave him
their highest award, the Legion of Honor.

In New York, people at Bergdorf Goodman department store glorified his work with a lavish display in their Fifth Avenue window.

But the attention made Bill squirm. He wanted the limelight on others, not himself.

Bill worked, having fun, until the end, June 25, 2016.

He was eighty-seven years old.

All over the world, people cried.

He invented street-fashion photography, said an admirer.

No one does it better than Bill, no one ever will.

And from Arthur Sulzberger Jr., his boss at *The New York Times*:
"We have lost a legend, and I am personally heartbroken to have lost a friend."

What wasn't lost,
what he left behind,
was his gift.

A lifetime of glorious pictures of clothes
and the power they lend us...

as we dress each day

for the runway

called life.

POLKA DOT PARADE: A BOOK ABOUT BILL CUNNINGHAM

AUTHOR'S NOTE

BY DEBORAH BLUMENTHAL

For someone who never cared about fame, Bill Cunningham was one of the most famous people in New York. The harder he tried to stay unfamous, the more famous he became.

Bill took pictures of stylish people for *The New York Times*, and people dressed to impress him. If Bill Cunningham wanted to take your picture, it proved you were cool.

For almost forty years, he would ride his bike to busy street corners and fancy parties and look for people who, like himself, had a passion for fashion. They and their creative costumes—feathers and leathers and furs and poufs and shawls and cowls—got into the newspaper, but in the end it was Bill who everyone remembered, not that he ever cared about that.

Nicholas Vreeland

Bill went to Harvard University on a scholarship, but dropped out after two months. He worked in women's clothing stores before designing hats, and then worked at newspapers, where he began taking pictures of people wearing outfits that he liked. He photographed old and young, rich and poor, men and women, boys, girls, even dogs, ducks, pythons, and monkeys, but only if they had a special look.

Sometimes he didn't even notice faces. When he once took a picture of a striking woman in a fur coat, beanie, and sunglasses, he didn't realize until later that she was Greta Garbo, one of the most famous actresses in the world.

I met Bill twice. Once at Lincoln Center before a concert. "Hello, kids," he said to me and my husband before heading off when some dash of flash in the distance caught his eye. The second time was at a party for my husband's book, *Stork Club*, at the New-York Historical Society, where guests wore Prohibition Era clothing. Bill liked the idea of taking pictures of people dressed up like dance girls and old-time gangsters.

William John Cunningham Jr. was born in Boston on March 13, 1929. He died in New York on June 25, 2016.

Bibliography

Bernstein, Jacob. "Bill Cunningham, Legendary *Times* Fashion Photographer, Dies at 87." *New York Times*, June 25, 2016. https://www.nytimes.com/2016/06/26/style/bill-cunningham-legendary-times-fashion-photographer-dies-at-87.html?_r=0.

Bill Cunningham New York. Film. Directed by Richard Press. 2010. New York City: Zeitgeist Films.

Kurdewan, John. "Bill Cunningham, Unpublished Photos." *New York Times*, December 16, 2016, https://www.nytimes.com/2016/12/16/fashion/bill-cunningham-unpublished-photos.html.

New York Times, Bill Cunningham archive, https://www.nytimes.com/by/bill-cunningham.

New York Times, Bill Cunningham "On the Street" video series, https://www.nytimes.com/video/on-the-street.

Notes

"He who seeks beauty will find it." Bill Cunningham New York.

"sheer poetry" Bill Cunningham, "On the Street; Postcard from Paris," *New York Times*, March 26, 2006, http://query.nytimes.com/gst/fullpage.html?res=9F06E7DA1730F935A15750C0A9609C8B63.

"with a dash of sapphire or violet" Lauren Collins, "Man on the Street: Bill Cunningham Takes Manhattan," *New Yorker*, March 16, 2009, http://www.newyorker.com/magazine/2009/03/16/man-on-the-street.

"I don't really see people—I see clothes." Collins, "Man on the Street."

"fashion is the armor to survive the reality of everyday life" Sophie Gallagher, "Bill Cunningham's Best Quotes on Style," *Harper's Bazaar Australia*, June 26, 2016, http://www.harpersbazaar.com.au/news/fashion-buzz/2016/6/bill-cunningham-dies-best-style-quotes/.

"A lot of people have taste, but they don't have the daring to be creative." Bill Cunningham New York.

Bill was a self-taught photographer. https://en.wikipedia.org/wiki/Bill_Cunningham_(American_photographer)

Fifth Avenue and Fifty-Seventh Street Jacob Bernstein, "New York City to Rename Intersection 'Bill Cunningham Corner'," *New York Times*, July 5, 2016, https://www.nytimes.com/2016/07/06/nyregion/bill-cunningham-corner-of-57th-street-and-fifth-avenue.html.

"My whole thing is to be invisible. You get more natural pictures that way too." "Bill Cunningham on Bill Cunningham," *New York Times*, June 25, 2016, https://www.nytimes.com/2016/06/26/fashion/bill-cunningham-on-his-life.html?ref=topics.

"an unbeatable combination" "First Thoughts about Bill Cunningham," June 8, 2016, first-thoughts.org/on/Bill+Cunningham/.

"I don't work. I only know how to have fun every day." Bill Cunningham New York.